Nessie
and Her Tisms

written by **Denise Sullivan Near**

illustrated by **Ashley Holden Hammond**

this book is **dedicated**

To my children, Kynzee, Harper, and Duke.

To my husband, Seth.

To our family and friends.

To everyone who has shown our family love and support.

And to all of the families who are navigating this same journey.

-Denise

First Edition Print 2019

Layout | Book Design | Cover Art by AshleyHoldenArt.com

Hi! My name is Nessie!
And I'd like you to know
a little bit about me.
Ok? So here I go.

I am on the spectrum
of Autism, you see.
And while you may have heard of this,
you still don't know me.

I am just a kid.
A kid, yes, just like you.
Even though I do some things
that might seem strange to you.

But there's always a good reason
that I do the things I do
and I'd like to take a minute
and explain it all to you.

See, when I'm nervous or excited,
or feeling overwhelmed within,
you might see me flap my hands,
or rock, or even spin.

And sometimes there's a noise
that you won't even hear,
but it's so loud to me
that it might hurt my ears!

A normal light in school
or headlights on a car,
they aren't too bright for you
but for me they really are!

With all my super senses
I should be a superhero!
But I'm not sure people see that . . .
if they only understood though!

And sometimes these things bug me
and other times they don't,
so it's really hard for me to know
when they will and when they won't.

SQUEAL!

I'm not always great
at telling people how I feel,
so my reaction to these things
is often a loud squeal.

A squeal can mean I'm happy!
Other times it means I'm sad.
And there are times that my squeal means
I'm really, really mad.

I see people stare
when I'm in a bad spot
and I wish that I knew how to say
that I'm just going through a lot.

Now please just take a moment
and pretend that you are me,
and no one really knows
what you hear and see.

The looks on people's faces
and the things they do and say,
that stuff makes perfect sense to you,
but to me, no, no way.

Like . . . I may not always look
when you say my name.
But don't give up on me,
I'm still glad you came!

I may not play your games
or join in right away,
but give me time, I'll come around,
just maybe not today!

Because I want to be your friend
but I also need my space.
You know how it feels
when people get right in your face!

So . . . while I may seem a little different
because of the few odd things I do,
let's be honest, ok?
You do some odd things too!

I call these odd things my "Tisms"
because they're just things that I do.
But there's so much more to me,
Just like there's so much more to you!

And I'm still figuring it all out,
learning day to day.
But we all are, right?
Just trying to find our way!

I am just a kid like you,
a little girl, Nessie.
And the only thing I know for sure
is I'm exactly who I'm supposed to be.

Look for more books about
Nessie, coming soon!

About the **author**

In December 2016, a few days before Christmas, Denise's daughter Harper was diagnosed with Autism. Harper was just two years old at the time. In that moment, as a million questions and fears raced through her mind, one thought in particular came to the forefront of all the others; she just wanted people, other children especially, to understand her daughter. That thought resonated with her as the days, weeks, and months passed. And soon, that thought became a mission and that mission became this book, "Nessie and Her Tisms."

Denise Sullivan Near is a Children's book author who turns her first-hand experience with her sweet little girl into a fun, very simply written, educational picture book. Through "Nessie and Her Tisms," Denise teaches young children about some of the unique behaviors of children on the spectrum by nurturing their natural curiosity. She is a mother, a wife, a writer, a Dental Hygienist and an Autism Awareness Advocate. She currently lives in Williamsport, Maryland with her husband Seth and three beautiful children, Kynzee, Harper and Duke.

About the **illustrator**

Ashley Holden Hammond is an illustrator, graphic designer, brand strategist, commercial artist and muralist. She holds a Bachelors from The Art Institute of Pittsburgh and has over 15 years of professional experience with multiple awards for design and fine art. Her paintings and caricatures have been printed and displayed in a variety of galleries and publications throughout the country. She lives in Hagerstown, Maryland with her husband Dustin, three sons, Dustin, Johnny and Dante, and their two dogs, Vinny and Fletcher. This is her first children's book but definitely not the last.

A big thank you

To all of the therapists and teachers who are dedicated
to improving the lives of children with Autism,
from the bottom of our hearts, thank you.